D-DAY

BEFORE AND AFTER

D-DAY

BEFORE AND AFTER

FOREWORD BY PHILIP HAMLYN WILLIAMS

With grateful thanks to Phil Hamlyn Williams
for his foreword and editorial contributions.

First published 2019
Reprinted 2019

The History Press
The Mill, Brimscombe Port
Stroud, Gloucestershire, GL5 2QG
www.thehistorypress.co.uk

© Mirrorpix, 2019

The right of Mirrorpix to be identified as the Author
of this work has been asserted in accordance with the
Copyright, Designs and Patents Act 1988.

British Library Cataloguing in Publication Data.
A catalogue record for this book is available from the British Library.

ISBN 978 0 7509 9066 0

Typesetting and origination by The History Press
Printed by Imak, Turkey

INTRODUCTION

D-Day is a story of audacious military planning coupled with great courage and individual commitment.

Many of the photographs in this book are of young men, far from all of whom would achieve old age. Most, certainly on the beaches on D-Day itself, were already old before their time, having seen active service in North Africa and the Mediterranean. These men had been chosen by their commanders for that very reason – a choice that caused great anguish to their loved ones at home.

A seaborne invasion was fraught with risk. Such had been attempted before, in North Africa and Sicily, but also at Anzio and Dieppe. Churchill surely was haunted by the landings at Gallipoli.

Yet, the most exhaustive preparations had been made. The invasion had been rehearsed. Some 300 million separate items of ordnance supplies had been packed, many by school children during their holidays. A massive fleet had been gathered together. Crucially, the RAF, in both Fighter and Bomber Command, had control of the air. The USA and Canada had provided thousands of men, tons of supplies and some of the best mechanical equipment in the form of the Sherman Tank and Jeep.

A carefully orchestrated plan of deception had left the Germans unsure of where the attack would come.

In the event the landings, on a scale never previously attempted, were achieved with fewer losses than feared, though some beaches fared far worse than others.

The bigger problems came when the troops advanced inland from the beaches. The Germans, by then, had had time to redeploy some of their key troops, although the insatiable demands of the eastern front were ever present. Stiff resistance was met, even from the war weary veterans. Caen, which features in a number of the photographs, had been targeted to fall on or soon after D-Day itself; in the event it took much longer.

The subsequent advance across France was gruelling. Max Hastings likened it to the battles of the previous wars; casualties were severe.

The experienced men and those who followed, who had spent sometimes years training for that moment, fought with commitment and courage. Questions, though, have subsequently been asked as to the effectiveness of their leaders. D-Day was always going to be a 'winner takes all' campaign. The Allies have every reason to be grateful that it was them; it could so easily have been otherwise.

Phil Hamlyn Williams

BEFORE D-DAY

▲ On 27 April 1944, His Majesty the King saw some of the troops who would take part in the liberation of Europe. During his tour he watched men putting the finishing touches to their training and also saw many of the surprises that awaited the enemy. This image shows King George VI inspecting the tank crews.

▲ The deserted villages of the South Devon coast are left battle-scarred and shattered after the area had been used as a 'battlefield' by American forces during their extensive invasion training. The previous December, 3,000 people, with all their belongings, were evacuated from village homes and cottages that for generations had been in their families, Now, with the departure of the troops, plans are being made for the people to return. Pictured is damage to a villa at Slapton, 21 July 1944.

▲ Valentine DD 'swimming' tanks leave the ramp of a landing craft and enter the sea about 3,000 yards from shore during a training exercise off the coast of Hayling Island, Hampshire ahead of the D-Day landings, 3 May 1944.

▲ On 1 June 1944, chief engineer Andy Duncan of Glasgow entertains the troops with his lightning sketches as they wait for departure for the D-Day landings.

◀ General Bernard Montgomery stands on the bonnet of a jeep as he addresses the troops during a pre D-Day inspection tour, 21 May 1944. Historian Max Hastings places great emphasis on the priority Montgomery gave to these visits and the very positive impact they had on morale.

◄ Supreme Command Allied Expeditionary Force meeting at Allied Headquarters prior to D-Day. From left to right: Lt General O.N. Bradley, Senior Commander American ground forces; Admiral Sir Bertram Ramsey, Allied Naval Commander; Air Chief Marshall Sir Arthur Tedder, Deputy Supreme Commander; General Dwight D. Eisenhower, Supreme Commander; General Sir Bernard Montgomery, C-in-C British armies; Air Chief Marshall Sir Trafford Leigh-Mallory, C-in-C Allied Expeditionary Air Force; Air Chief Lt General E.W. Bedell Smith.

➤ This picture was taken during an exercise of invasion craft and men taking part in the great assault. It shows vehicles disembarking from a Rhino Ferry, which has transported them from a landing ship anchored off the beach, 1 June 1944.

HOBART'S FUNNIES

Hobart's Funnies were a number of unusually modified tanks operated by the 79th Armoured Division and the Royal Engineers. These specialised tanks were developed under the guidance of Major General Percy Hobart to overcome the problems of the planned invasion of Normandy. They played a major part on the Commonwealth beaches during the landings and are the forerunners of the modern combat engineering vehicles we see on today's battlefields. All of these images date from *c*. 1 June 1944.

▲ A modified Churchill tank with a small box girder – an assault bridge that was carried in front of the tank and could be dropped to span a 30ft gap in thirty seconds.

⋀ A modified Churchill tank after crossing a fascine.

◀ A modified Churchill tank using a fascine – a bundle of wooden poles or rough brushwood lashed together with wires carried in front of the tank that could be released to fill a ditch or form a step. Metal pipes in the centre of the fascine allowed water to flow through it.

▲ People in East Ham have been working together to provide a worthwhile send-off for troops passing through their district to embark for France. Money has been raised to provide cigarettes, drinks and food. Some people have contributed their weeks' rations. Housewives are cutting sandwiches; the children are helping to wash up. RAOC man John Frost, or Frosty as he was known, recalled the journey round the North Circular, with crowds of people waving flags and offering cups of tea as the convoy made its slow passage. It also passed the Ford factory at Dagenham, where the workers had rigged up a banner bearing the words 'Good Luck Boys'.

ON D-DAY

▲ British glider-borne troops march out to board their craft for take-off in the first wave of the airborne attack on German defences in Normandy. On the night of 5 June 1944 a force of 181 men, led by Major John Howard, took off from RAF Tarrant Rushton in Dorset, southern England in six Horsa gliders to capture Pegasus Bridge, and also Horsa Bridge, a few hundred yards to the east, over the Orne River.

➤ British paratroopers of 22 Independent Parachute Company, British 6th Airborne Division at RAF Harwell wait to board the Armstrong Whitworth Albemarle Mk V that will drop them over Normandy at the start of the D-Day offensive. Their faces have been blackened and they are wearing camouflage helmets.

◄ British and American airborne troops and parachutists landed behind German defences at around 1.30 a.m. on 6 June 1944.

➤ Hamilcar gliders of the British Army 6th Airborne Division used during the invasion are seen coming in to land in Ranville, Normandy, bringing with them the Tetrarch tanks of 6th Airborne Division's armoured reconnaissance regiment, on the evening of 6 June 1944.

◄ Airborne troops of 6th Airborne Infantry Brigade admire the graffiti chalked on the side of their Horsa glider at an RAF airfield in England as they prepare to fly out to Normandy as reinforcements for the 6th Airborne Division's second lift on the evening of the D-Day landings.

▲ D-Day glider pilots Peter Boyle and Geoff Parkways' glider (*centre*) where it landed at Pegasus Bridge.

▲ Following the D-Day landings in Northern France during the Second World War, Horsa gliders are pictured besides the Pegasus bridge over the Caen Canal at Benouville in Normandy, the first to land in France on the day of the Allied invasion.

➤ American troops wade through the water beside amphibious tanks and fighting equipment as they surge ashore to storm Nazi defences during the initial landings in France. Soldiers and vehicles previously landed can be seen moving forward on the beachhead.

▶ American paratroopers
file along with full
equipment to board their
transport plane for the
allied invasion of Nazi
occupied Europe on D-Day.

➤ Part of the British invasion fleet bound for the Gold, Juno and Sword Normandy beaches, seen here on the morning of D-day from the cliffs overlooking Folkestone. Destroyers of the Royal Navy lay a smoke screen to hide the fleet from the French coast.

▲ In the early hours of the morning of 6 June naval ships carried out an intense bombardment of the coastal defences, many of which had been put in place over the preceding few months as the German High Command braced itself for the invasion which they knew was coming; what they didn't know was where. For this reason, RAF bombers and fighter bombers attacked not only the Normandy beach defences but those elsewhere along the French coast.

▲ British army commandos of No. 4 Commando, 1st Special Service Brigade, prime grenades ready for going ashore.

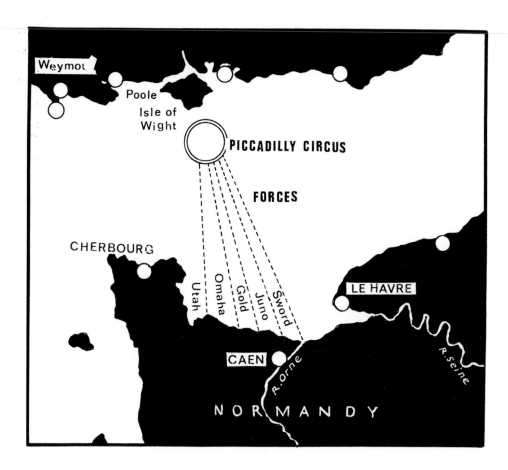

Weymou

Poole

Isle of
Wight

PICCADILLY CIRCUS

FORCES

CHERBOURG

Utah Omaha Gold Juno Sword

LE HAVRE

CAEN

R.orne

R.seine

N O R M A N D Y

▲ The planning for D-Day began in 1943 and was an exhaustive process involving a great many people. Thousands of maps were produced under great secrecy and amazingly remained secret until the invasion took place. This is an illustration of the route the invasion force took to the beaches of Normandy on D-Day. Of the five beaches, Omaha and Utah were allocated as to the USA, Gold to the British, Juno to the British and Canadians and Sword to the British.

▲ The gigantic fleet of warships, transports, landing craft and supply ships waits for the signal to launch the assault for the liberation of Europe.

◄ An army artillery officer works with a Royal Navy gunner officer to plot the next barrage on enemy positions in Normandy. The guns of the Royal Navy's cruisers and battleships helped to subdue enemy fire during the first few weeks of Operation Overlord.

▲ Landing craft loaded with troops head towards the Normandy beaches during the D-Day invasion.

▲ Part of the invasion fleet lying off the Normandy beaches for Operation Overlord.

◄ Climbing out of a Landing Craft – Vehicle Personnel (LCVP), US troops board a Landing Craft – Infantry (LCI(L)) during embarkation for the invasion of the Nazi's 'Fortress Europe'. Navy men help with battle gear.

▲ D-Day landings on the beaches of Normandy. The image shows what looks like a Hobart's Funny (see p. 16).

▲ US troops waiting to disembark.

◀ Canadian Troops landing in France on D-Day.

▼ British and Allied troops on the beaches of Normandy after the D-Day landings.

▲ Troops of 3rd Infantry Division land on Queen Red beach, Sword area, early on 6 June 1944, the first British formation to land at Sword Beach. In the foreground are sappers of 84 Field Company Royal Engineers, part of No. 5 Beach Group, identified by the white bands around their helmets. Behind them, medical orderlies of 8 Field Ambulance, RAMC, can be seen assisting wounded men. In the background commandos of 1st Special Service Brigade can be seen disembarking from their small landing craft (LCI(S)).

▲ Allied troops take shelter behind their vehicles as German shells pound a French beach on 6 June 1944.

▶ American infantry moves forward from the Normandy beaches shortly after the D-Day landings.

▶ Endless streams of American troops move up the beaches.

◄ Troops of the Canadian 9th Infantry Brigade part of 3rd Division carrying their bicycles ashore from landing craft LCL 299 in the Nan White Sector of Juno Beach shortly after midday on 6 June 1944.

▲ The scene on the eastern extremity of Sword beach as soldiers of the 1st Special Service Brigade proceed inland under shell, mortar and sniper fire.

▲ Liberation of Europe. Scenes on a Normandy beachhead as crack British troops made their first landing on the morning on Tuesday, 6 June 1944. You can see artillery setting up on the beach to protect the landing troops.

▲ British beach group troops and Red Cross personnel wade ashore from landing craft on Queen beach, Sword area, to join their comrades who made the initial assaults on the beaches earlier in the day.

▲ British troops under fire on Juno beach at Normandy, soon after zero hour. The German aircraft visible in the sky over the beach has just bombed a house, now in flames. In the foreground is a column of German prisoners just captured. The RAF were firmly in evidence with fighter planes to protect the troops from such attacks, some of which inevitably slipped through.

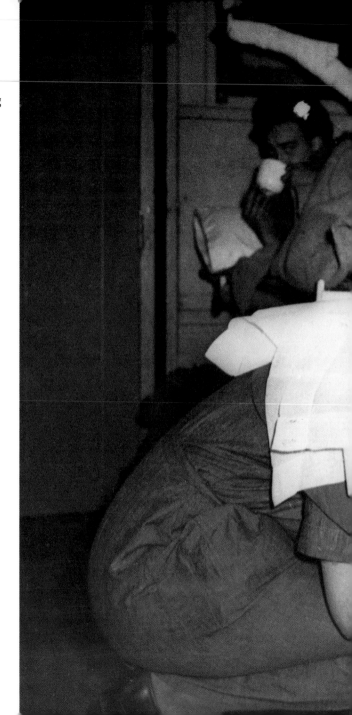

▶ Wounded British troops on board the hospital train, following the successful Allied invasion of Northern France. Pictured here is Marine G. Sincock of Manchester receiving a drink from a sister.

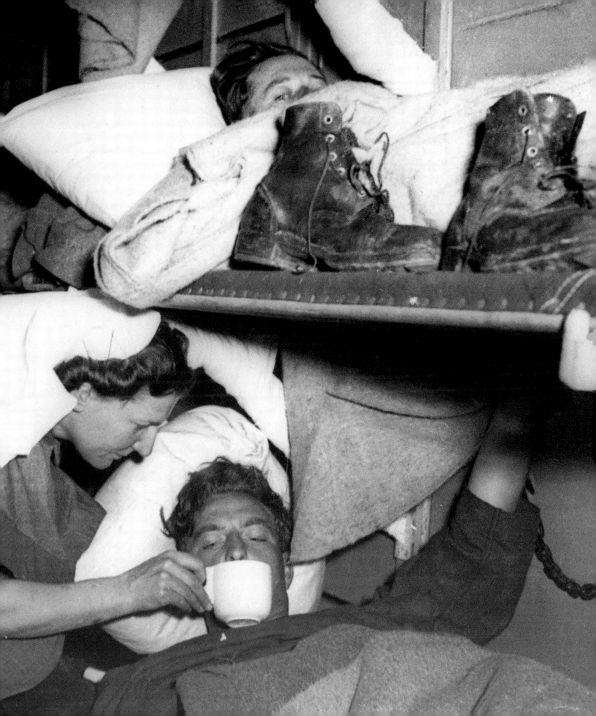

▲ British troops wounded in the D-Day assault on Normandy are pictured on their arrival back in Britain. Pictured here are, from left to right: Corporal Stott of Yeadon, Leeds; Trooper G. Gart of Kent; and Lance Bombadier F.B. Adhead of Walsall.

➤ Battle-weary German prisoners shelter in one of their own beach defence trenches while waiting to be marched to a prisoner-of-war camp in France. They were amongst the first to be captured by the Allied Expeditionary Force during the D-Day landings in France.

▲ German prisoners of war disembark from a large landing craft (LCI(L)-500) and begin the march to a temporary prison camp on one of the Gold area beaches.

▲ Badly battered German gunner of a gun nest on beach of Northern France, staggers out of under-ground net under watchful eye of a burley U.S Army MP, 10 June 1944.

⌃ A short service in progress at St Anne's Church in Manchester after news of the successful landings in Normandy.

▲ A chaplain leading a Sunday service aboard the HMS *Scylla* shortly after D-Day while she was in anchor, still off the Normandy coast, 11 June 1944.

▲ Loudspeakers at the Army Equipment Exhibition in Manchester announces news of the successful landings in Normandy, Northern France.

CAEN

▲ British reinforcements land on Gold beach on 16 June 1944 for the big push into the Normandy town of Caen. The plan had been for Caen to be taken on or soon after D-Day itself. In the event the whole of June passed without any success.

▲ British commando troops passing through a town near Caen heading inland into Northern France on the mission to liberate France and Europe, shortly after the Normandy landings.

▲ A British army DUKW amphibious vehicle passes through the Normandy village of Courseulles-sur-Mer during the push towards Caen.

▲ Transport moves across the the Caen Canal Bridge (later renamed the Pegasus Bridge), 8 June 1944. This lifting bridge over the Caen Canal at Benouville was captured on D-Day by British glider-borne troops of the 6th Airborne Division, whose machines crash-landed close to the canal bank.

➤ Vehicles including a Royal Signals jeep and trailer and an RASC Leyland lorry move across Pegasus Bridge on 9 June 1944. Signallers are seen fixing telephone lines across the bridge. Thousands of telegraph poles and fixings had been brought across in the expectation that communications would have been destroyed.

▼ British reinforcements land on Gold beach for the big push into the Normandy town of Caen, 16 June 1944 (pp. 80–82).

▲ Troops enjoy a cup of tea and a spot of lunch, taking a break from offloading reinforcements on Gold Beach, Normandy, on 16 June 1944.

▲ Churchill Tanks and infantry advance across a cornfield on 28 June 1944, part of the fiercely-fought British attack between Tilly and Caen. Extensive gaps have been made in the enemy lines.

CHERBOURG

⋀ The bombardment of Cherbourg. Ships from the United States Navy and the British Royal Navy attacked German fortifications in and near the city, firing in support of US Army units that were engaged in the Battle of Cherbourg. HMS *Glasgow* emerges from a smoke screen with her battle ensign flying from the foremast on 25 June 1944. Censors have removed the radar on the ships in this image.

➤ This picture, taken from HMS *Enterprise* on 25 June 1944, shows, from left to right: United States destroyer ships USS *Nevada* and USS *Quincy*; another unidentified destroyer; and HMS *Glasgow* of the British Royal Navy. Censors have removed the radar on the ships in this image.

▲ The advance on Cherbourg. A column of German prisoners is marched from the town.

▲ German soldiers captured in Cherbourg are escorted to a prisoner-of-war camp by Allied forces, 30 June 1944.

▲ In mid June, the Allies were widening the wedge across the Cherbourg Peninsula, where several German troops were believed to be trapped. This image shows Allied troops constructing slit trenches, a necessity due to the closely wooded country of the Touffreveille.

THE BATTLE FOR FRANCE

▲ British commandos who landed on D-Day had clear first objectives: capture a gun site, disposing of enemy snipers on their way, before, with the aid of tanks, reaching and capturing the battery. Here, in pursuit of this goal, men of Number 46 Commando, 4th Special Service Brigade, pass through the village of Douvres la Delivrande on 8 June 1944. French civilians look on.

▲ Following a terrific barrage by massed field guns, British forces opened an attack in the neighbourhood of Tilly on 26 June, and considerable breaches were made in the enemy lines. The action was very fierce, with house-to-house fighting in the surrounding villages. Large numbers of tanks were employed by both sides. This picture was taken during the first wave of the assault and it shows British troops in a sunken lane firing on enemy held positions on the outskirts of a village near Tilly, Normandy.

▲ British soldiers of 12th Parachute Battalion, 5th Parachute Brigade and 6th Airborne Division enjoy a cup of tea after fighting their way back to their own lines near Ranville, after three days behind enemy lines engaged in a guerilla war with Germany army soldiers, 10 June 1944.

↑ Lorries and jeeps driving off the Mulberry harbour at Gold Beach, Arromanches, 12 June 1944. A Mulberry was a prefabricated harbour. Over 8,000 men worked for eight months to build these floating structures, which in addition to the vast quantities of concrete used 110,000 tonnes of steel and weighed nearly a million tonnes when completed.

▲ A powerful shovel tackles the seemingly hopeless task of clearing the streets of the Normandy town of Valognes of debris, 30 June 1944. Allied shelling had levelled many buildings before the Nazi's fled.

◄ Canadian troops rest under a hedge in the Normandy countryside following bitter close-quarter combat with the Germans, 1 July 1944. The sunken roads and hedges of Normandy (known locally as the bocage) made ambush tactics easier and therefore favoured the German defenders, making the Allied advance difficult.

◄ A soldier visits the graves of his British comrades who have been killed during the fighting in Normandy. They were buried by French civilians who have also placed flowers on the graves.

▲ Forward Observation Bombardment men at work, among whom are many naval telegraphists and volunteers from HM Ships. The gun crews of the Royal Navy rely on them for correct ranges as they bombard enemy strongpoints and gun nests ashore.

▲ British troops in Sherman Tanks roll through the narrow cobbled streets of a Normandy town, 5 July 1944.

▲ British troops are pictured talking to a local gendarme in a Normandy town, 5 July 1944.

▲ American troops in jeeps make their way through a bomb-damaged Normandy town.

HINDENBURG

UNDER NEW MANAGEMENT

Sgt. SAVAGE

AND HIS CHINDITS

▲ A Bofors gun crew of the British army celebrate after capturing the Hindenburg Bastion, 6 July 1944. This was a huge concrete emplacement with trench communications, one of the most formidable strongpoints they had to overcome after storming Germany's much-vaunted 'West Wall'.

▲ With an improvement of the weather off the Normandy beaches, unloading from various craft is in full swing on 9 June 1944.

▲ Troops, tanks, vehicles and stores are unloaded on the Normandy beaches. Behind them more and more ships are waiting their turn to unload.

◄▲ Unloading from a liberty ship to an LCT is in progress on 10 July 1944, as supplies and reinforcements arrive on the beaches of Normandy for the troops.

▲ British troops unloading a ship on the beaches of Normandy, 10 July 1944.

▲ Artillery men of a medium battery in action in Normandy, 25 July 1944. They are laying down special tracks on one of the roads leading to the front.

▲ RAF ground crews on an airstrip in Normandy after the Liberation of Europe.

▲ Wearied by house-to-house fighting in a French coastal town, American troops take a break in a milk house, part of a farm that was cleared of German snipers before moving on to the next objective.

➤ Canadian troops flank a closely-packed Allied convoy moving inland after the early landings on the French coast, 8 June 1944.

▲ American soldiers of the 4th Division Command, by General Lighting Joe Collins, seen here during the attack on Cherbourg.

▲ The D-Day invasion of Normandy, France. British troops about to pass through a village after the landings, c. 10 June 1944.

▲ A Sherman VC Firefly Tank of 24th Lancers, 8th Armoured Brigade, near St Leger, 11 June 1944. The Sherman Firefly was based on the US M4 Sherman Tank but fitted with the powerful 3-inch calibre British 17-pounder anti-tank gun as its main weapon by the British Army as a stopgap until future British tank designs came into service, the Sherman Firefly became the most common vehicle with the 17-pounder in the war.

▲ Winston Churchill visiting Normandy in jeep with cigar in mouth, 12 June 1944.
Wearing his nautical uniform, Churchill travelled by Army jeep into the hinterland. All
around were the signs of recent fighting - wrecked buildings and vehicles, crashed gliders
and aircraft, corpses of men.

▲ Winston Churchill seen here in deep conversation with Admiral Ramsay on their way to the Mulberry harbour on Sword Beach.

◄ Winston Churchill lands on the Mulberry harbour on Sword Beach for a tour of inspection of the Normandy Bridgehead, on 12 June 1944, fourteen days after the D-Day Landings.

◀ Winston Churchill lands on the Mulberry harbour on Sword Beach for a tour of inspection of the Normandy Bridgehead 6 days after the D-Day Landings, June 1944.

▼ Field Marshal Bernard Montgomery with Prime Minister Winston Churchill during a tour of the Normandy Bridgehead, following the invasion of Northern France by Allied forces in June 1944.

▲ Germans, former 'Herrenvolk', come over the crest of a hill with their hands over their heads in surrender and are rounded up by American soldiers, one of whom can be seen at the extreme right of the picture, 13 June 1944.

➤ American soldiers of a shore fire control party set up shop in an old shell hole and immediately proceed to direct the fire of naval guns against the targets on the beach, 13 June 1944.

▲ Gliders of the British Army 6th Airborne Division, used during the invasion, are scattered about on a vast glider field north of Ranville, 15 June 1944.

▲ British soldier with a squirrel on his arm at a Normandy port in Northern France shortly after the D-Day landings began the Allied invasion of the continent during the Second World War, 16 June 1944.

▲ British troops on the anti-aircraft gun in a Normandy town in Northern France, 16 June 1944.

The board reads (as visible):

The DERBY ~ 1944
1½ MILE

HORSE	JOCKEY	WIN	PLACE
	SMITH	14-1	7-2
	RICHARDS	16-1	4-1
	LITTLEWOOD	33-1	8-1
		14-1	7-2
	RICHARDS	10-1	3-1
	WRAGG	12-1	3-1
	RICHARDS	4-1	EVENS
		30-1	10-1
		10-1	10-1
		33-1	8-1
		6-1	6-4
		40-1	10-1
		5-1	3-1
	UTTER	50-1	12-1
	SMITH	3-1	6-4
	LANE	16-1	4-1
	M. BEARY	33-1	8-1
	EVANS	20-1	5-1
	SIMPSON	40-1	10-1
	T. CAREY	12-1	3-1
	WESTON	16-1	4-1
	NEVETT	20-1	5-1
	RICHARDS	14-1	6-1
	DONOGHUE		6-4

AND
STARTING
KEEP YOUR

▲ British troops observing Derby Day, 18 June 1944 – if only on a small scale, due to other ongoing urgent duties. Wherever possible, amateur bookmakers set up their stalls and anyone who cared to take the risk became an 'amateur bookmaker' or 'Sweepstake promoter'. Here Sergeant A.A. Dalziel of the Royal Corps of Signals is the bookmaker and Lance Corporal Day is his clerk. They did a roaring business beside the board showing the horses and jockeys. The result was received on the camp radio.

▲ British tank crew are having a rest, sleeping under the protection of their tank, 17 June 1944. RAOC man John Frost slept under his mobile ordnance store on a stretcher he had borrowed.

▲ The first American casualty to reach England following the Allied invasion of occupied Europe is lifted from an aeroplane by medics. The wounded paratrooper received a small-arms wound in the head from enemy fire during the landings.

✦ American wounded from the Normandy beaches arrive at an undisclosed British port on the south coast, 9 June 1944.

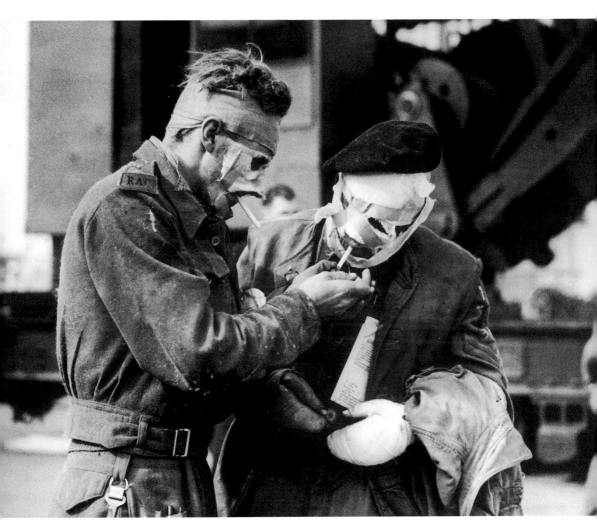

▲ Two soldiers, casualties of the Normandy Landings, enjoy a cigarette after disembarking from the hospital ship, 12 June 1944.

▲ American Red Cross Nurses on their way to the battle at the River Seine travel in the back of Army trucks through the town of La Loupe, 45 miles west of Paris.

▲ Personnel of Queen Alexandra's Imperial Military Nursing Service (QAIMNS) were the first women to arrive in Northern France following the Normandy Landings. On 13 June, seven days after the landings, Lieutenant Colonel Helm of Colchester arrived with two sisters, followed by a party of another fifty nurses three days later. Here the Matron, Senior Commander Mellor, addresses the nurses and details them for their duties, 16 June 1944.

▲ The sisters sleep in the open air in slit trenches to be safe from bombing. Here they are seen carrying their blankets to the trenches, 16 June 1944.

▲ Royal Army Medical Corps (RAMC) and QAIMNS nurses carry out a wounded soldier after he received attention in the operating theatre, 16 June 1944.

◄ A general view of a beach in France, three weeks after D-Day, showing the constant flow of supplies being unloaded from the many cargo ships lying off shore, 27 June 1944.

▲ Prime Minister Winston Churchill pictured visited Normandy six weeks after the Allied D-day landings. Here he is seen meeting British soldiers on 23 July 1944.

➤ Lance Corporal E. Martin, a military policeman, sits astride his motorcycle as he chats to Corporal Joyce Collins of Norwich and Lance Corporal Celia Strong of Plumstead, of the ATS, both of whom will act as MPs in Normandy, at 21st Army Group HQ, 28 July 1944.

➤ The first arrivals of the ATS in Normandy, Northern France, attached to the 21st, surrounded by troops anxious to know the latest news from England, 28 July 1944.

◄ Living in trenches built by the routed German defenders of the beaches, these Liverpool gunners are now manning anti-aircraft guns against German attacks aimed at hindering the disembarkation of Allied supplies on the beaches, 4 September 1944. They have christened their new abode 'Merseyside'.

"S-S-Stop s-s-saying 'S-S-Say W-When'!"

▲ *Daily Mirror* readers, seeing the calendar sheet behind Hitler in this cartoon, wrote in after D-Day to ask how 'Zec' knew the date three weeks ahead, 21 April 1944.